Greater Than a Tourist Book Series Reviews from ...

I think the series is wonderful and beneficial for tourists to get information before visiting the city.
-Seckin Zumbul, Izmir Turkey

I am a world traveler who has read many trip guides but this one really made a difference for me. I would call it a heartfelt creation of a local guide expert instead of just a guide.
-Susy, Isla Holbox, Mexico

New to the area like me, this is a must have!
-Joe, Bloomington, USA

This is a good series that gets down to it when looking for things to do at your destination without having to read a novel for just a few ideas.
-Rachel, Monterey, USA

Good information to have to plan my trip to this destination.
-Pennie Farrell, Mexico

Aptly titled, you won't just be a tourist after reading this book. You'll be greater than a tourist!
-Alan Warner, Grand Rapids, USA

Thank you for a fantastic book.
-Don, Philadelphia, USA
Great ideas for a port day.
-Mary Martin USA

Michelle Torres

Even though I only have three days to spend in San Miguel in an upcoming visit, I will use the author's suggestions to guide some of my time there. An easy read - with chapters named to guide me in directions I want to go.
-Robert Catapano, USA

Great insights from a local perspective! Useful information and a very good value!
-Sarah, USA

This series provides an in-depth experience through the eyes of a local. Reading these series will help you to travel the city in with confidence and it'll make your journey a unique one.
-Andrew Teoh, Ipoh, Malaysia

Tourists can get an amazing "insider scoop" about a lot of places from all over the world. While reading, you can feel how much love the writer put in it.
-Vanja Živković, Sremski Karlovci, Serbia

GREATER THAN A TOURIST –

SALAMANCA

SPAIN

50 Travel Tips from a Local

Michelle Torres

Michelle Torres

Cover designed by: Lisa Rusczyk Ed. D.
Image: https://pixabay.com/en/salamanca-spain-cathedral-261510/

Greater Than a Tourist
Visit our website at www.GreaterThanaTourist.com

Lock Haven, PA
All rights reserved.
ISBN: 9781973413301

>TOURIST

50 TRAVEL TIPS FROM A LOCAL

Michelle Torres

BOOK DESCRIPTION

Are you excited about planning your next trip?

Do you want to try something new?

Would you like some guidance from a local?

If you answered yes to any of these questions, then this Greater Than a Tourist book is for you.

Greater than a Tourist – Salamanca, Spain by Michelle Torres offers the inside scoop on Salamanca. Most travel books tell you how to travel like a tourist. Although there is nothing wrong with that, as part of the Greater Than a Tourist series, this book will give you travel tips from someone who has lived at your next travel destination.

In these pages you'll discover advice that will help you throughout your stay. This book will not tell you exact addresses or store hours but instead will give you excitement and knowledge from a local that you may not find in other smaller print travel books.

Travel like a local. Slow down, stay in one place, and get to know the people and the culture. By the time you finish this book, you will be eager and prepared to travel to your next destination.

Michelle Torres

TABLE OF CONTENTS

Michelle Torres

ABOUT THE AUTHOR

Michelle is a Venezuelan currently living in Salamanca, Spain. She fell instantly in love with the city and its history. Since she arrived, she's been almost obsessed with the details of Salamanca; there are so many things to see and enjoy in such a tiny city.

Even though she wasn't born as a "Charra", there's an old saying that says that anyone can be Charro, no matter where you come from. So, if you fall in love like she did, consider yourself a Salamantine as well.

She loves walking through the city, having a nice cup of black coffee, reading books and, mostly, learning new things.

Michelle Torres

HOW TO USE THIS BOOK

The Greater Than a Tourist book series was written by someone who has lived in an area for over three months. The goal of this book is to help travelers either dream or experience different locations by providing opinions from a local. The author has made suggestions based on their own experiences. Please do your own research before traveling to the area in case the suggested places are unavailable.

Michelle Torres

FROM THE PUBLISHER

Traveling can be one of the most important parts of a person's life. The anticipation and memories that you have are some of the best. As a publisher of the Greater Than a Tourist book series, as well as the popular 50 Things to Know book series, we strive to help you learn about new places, spark your imagination, and inspire you. Wherever you are and whatever you do I wish you safe, fun, and inspiring travel.

Lisa Rusczyk Ed. D.
CZYK Publishing

Michelle Torres

OUR STORY

Traveling is a passion of the "Greater than a Tourist" series creator. Lisa studied abroad in college, and for their honeymoon Lisa and her husband toured Europe. During her travels to Malta, an older man tried to give her some advice based on his own experience living on the island since he was a young boy. She was not sure if she should talk to the stranger but was interested in his advice. When traveling to some places she was wary to talk to locals because she was afraid that they weren't being genuine. Through her travels, Lisa learned how much locals had to share with tourists. Lisa created the "Greater Than a Tourist" book series to help connect people with locals. A topic that locals are very passionate about sharing.

Michelle Torres

INTRODUCTION

"Salamanca, that bewitches the will to return to it
upon all who the gentleness of its home have liked."
Miguel de Cervantes

Salamanca is the capital of Salamanca state, inside the Castilla y León Community, in Spain. This is a small (about 40 km2) but gorgeous city filled with history. Its origins go back to 2700 years ago, so every step you take will be on millennial streets. Its Old Town was declared World Heritage Site in 1988, and was the European Capital of Culture in 2002. It's well known for its university (USAL, founded in 1218) and foreigners come here to learn Spanish. People born in Salamanca are commonly known as "charros".

You can arrive here by train or bus from Madrid. It's a 2-3 hour trip, I recommend you to take the train to enjoy the view of the towns on your way here. When it comes to staying, there are many options: Airbnb, 5 stars hotel or hostals with room-sharing (adventurous opportunity to meet other travelers if you're traveling alone). No matter what you like, pick one as close to the Plaza Mayor as possible. It's the heart of the city, so you'll have everything at walking distance.

Salamanca has a public airport close to Matacán city, but is available in certain moments of the year.

Michelle Torres

1. BASICS OF SALAMANCA

As almost every city in Spain, the working hours in Salamanca are from 9-10 AM to 2 PM and from 4 PM to 9-10 PM. Take this into consideration if you want to go shopping or visit stores. Check their schedule. On Sundays, most shops close. Some restaurants and museums are opened.

Any time of the year is amazing for visiting Salamanca. The patrimony, culture, and gastronomy are always for the disposal of tourists. Charros are very gentle and sweet people, so if you get lost or have doubts about how to get somewhere, don't be afraid and ask!

Here, the weather is Mediterranean. Winter (from December to February) is cold with low temperatures, so if you visit in this time of the year, don't forget to bring winter clothes. Summer is usually filled with students learning Spanish, and the temperatures are usually above 30 degrees Celsius. Keep these things in mind while you're planning your visit.

From now on, I'll walk you through the places to visit, eat and where to enjoy the best of what Salamanca has to offer!

2. HAVE DINNER IN THE PLAZA MAYOR

This square is literally the heart of Salamanca. Its main structure was built from 1729 to 1756, in a Baroque style. In 1935 was declared "National Monument", for being the most decorated, proportionate and harmonic square of its time, and declared "Artistic National Monument" in 1973. Most of the places you'll visit will be around this Plaza, and some references will be like: "x place is 5 minutes walking from the Plaza Mayor". At daylight it's beautiful, but at night this place is stunning. Depending on the time of the year you visit, you can watch performances, concerts, or visit fairs there.

There are lots of restaurants and cafes in the square to sit and enjoy the view. I strongly recommend you to dine on the terrace of any restaurant (to sit on the square itself), to have wine and chat while enjoying the square at night. In case you get too distracted, the bell of the clock will sound every hour to let you know how long you've been there.

3. Tormes' River

This river has been the main witness to the history of the city. Salamanca was born and grew around its riversides. It has inspired famous stories, such as "El Lazarillo de Tormes" (The Blind Man's Guide of Tormes), and famous authors, like Miguel de Cervantes, Lope De Vega, Saint Teresa of Avila, among others.

Nowadays, in certain times of the year you can rent a boat on its shore and tour the river for one hour. There are plenty of ducks swimming on it. It's amazing to see them flying or swimming with the landscape of the city, the river, and the bridge.

If you like fishing, you can do that as well. There are mostly trouts and carps. If you want to, you have to ask for permission in the Town's Hall with anticipation.

4. FIND THE FROG

The University of Salamanca is one of the most famous buildings to visit in the city. It's the oldest University in Spain, founded in 1218. It has gorgeous and valuable things to see. You can't say you visited Salamanca if you didn't go to the University.

The carvings of the University's walls have lots of symbols, but the frog is the one you're looking for. If you look carefully, you'll find it sitting on top of a skull.

Its history goes back to the construction of the University. Its meaning isn't very clear, but one of the stories says that it was carved by the artist as a reminder for students. Back then, the students were only men, so this was a warning for them, to avoid partying, alcohol and mostly prostitutes. They had to focus on their books and grades instead of the worldly pleasures. The frog meant lust, so "if you fall into the sin of lust, you will die". The message was quite straightforward, right?

Nowadays, tradition says that finding the frog without help will bring good fortune and students will pass their tests. You can't say you visited Salamanca if you didn't look for it.

5. THE SKY INSIDE A VAULT

Back then, the University was divided into different schools. The "minor schools" were the ones where people went to study high school. The construction of those "minor schools" started in 1428. In 1931 they were declared a Historical Heritage Site. As you walk across its arches, you'll get a hint of what it was like to be a high school student back then.

In one of the classrooms (now a museum), is a painting made by Fernando Gallego at the end of the XV century, called "El Cielo de Salamanca" (Salamanca's Sky). It was originally on the library's roof but after a fire in the XVIII century, a new vault was built, destroying two-thirds of these paintings. The remains were found in the XX century, hidden 4 meters above the new vault. Once restored, the paintings were relocated where they are now.

The painting represents the zodiacal constellations of Leo, Virgo, Libra, Scorpio, and Sagittarius, as well as other constellations like Hercules, the Hydra, the Centaur, the Crow, the Crown and the Snake. Also, there's a representation of the Sun sitting in a chariot pulled by horses, and another of the god Mercury, sitting in a chariot pulled by two eagles. It's basically a synopsis of the wisdom and the tradition of the time about astronomy and astrology.

Michelle Torres

6. THE OLD CATHEDRAL

You can see it almost anywhere you're standing in the city. Even though it looks like one big cathedral, they're actually two.

The Old Cathedral was built between the XII and XII centuries. If you're an art fan, you'll see the combinations of Romanesque and Gothic styles. When the New Cathedral was being planned, the Old one was almost destroyed. But back then, people needed somewhere to celebrate the cult while the New was being constructed, so the Old Cathedral remained.

Its walls are spectacular, and inside you'll surround yourself with different epochs of art. In the Big Chapel, you'll see artworks from the XV to the XX centuries. There are also little chapels and a cloister.

You can have a tour inside. The price per person is 4,75€. Includes a tour of the Old and the New Cathedrals, the cloister, the museum, and an audio guide. There are discounts for kids and large groups.

7. THE NEW CATHEDRAL

It was built between XVI and XVIII centuries. The styles present are the Late Gothic, Renaissance, and Baroque. Its southern wall backs up the north of the Old Cathedral. It's the second biggest cathedral in Spain.

Back in 1755, the New Cathedral was severely damaged by the Lisbon earthquake. Those cracks still remain upon its walls. As well as the Old, the New has chapels to tour and a choir. Light enters through hundreds of windows, enhancing the experience.

The most interesting part of this cathedral, besides its history, is probably a craving on one of its walls. If you look carefully, you'll see a carving of an astronaut. What is it doing in a Cathedral built centuries ago? If that's not enough, next to it is a dragon having ice cream. The myth says that it was made by aliens centuries ago. Skeptics affirm they belong to a restoration made in 1992. Whichever you want to believe, the Cathedral is a must.

8. IERONIMUS' EXPOSITION

The "Ieronimus" is the name of the exposition where you visit the Cathedral's Towers.

You'll be able to see the Cathedrals from the inside, the outside and have a view of the city on 30 meters above the ground. The one hour tour will walk you through different rooms and terraces, where the view is unique. In every floor, you'll see an exposition of objects, instruments, even letters or religious relics.

There's also a night guided visit, called "While The Cathedral Sleeps".

If you have the opportunity to go, don't miss it, is absolutely worth it. You'll fall in love with the city if you haven't already.

9. TOUR THE CITY IN THE TRAIN

This "train" will drive you through the important streets of Salamanca. It starts in Anaya Square, in front of the Cathedral. The route takes about 30 minutes. You'll see the city in a comfortable seat, just have your camera prepared for the pictures.

If you don't like the train-plan, you can hire a tourist guide. In the tourist office (located in Plaza Mayor) they'll assist you with which tour-plan suits you and your group the most: through monuments, a night tour, or maybe learn about legends, or watch theatrical performances... You can walk the city and know its history in any way.

If you like independence throughout your visit, there's an app for mobile and tablets to download for free. You can use it as a reference when touring the city.

For the train, adults pay 3,50 €, kids 1,75€. There are group discounts and you can rent it for private events as well.

10. Walk On The Roman Bridge

This bridge was built in the Roman empire. Yes, two millennia ago. It crosses the Tormes river, considered one of the most dangerous rivers back then. It was the only access to the city until the early XX century and has been restored a lot of times throughout the centuries, after devastating floods and wars. It's one of the main symbols of the city, with a representation in Salamanca's shield. The legend says it was built by Hercules and restored by the Roman emperor Trajan in the 1st century.

There's a sculpture of a boar at the entrance of the bridge (the oldest sculpture of Salamanca). Apparently, it was made in the Iron Age by the vettones. It's also included in the shield of the city, walking on the bridge.

It was declared Artistic Monument in 1931. Now is destined for pedestrians only. The view of the city is stunning from here, don't forget to bring your camera!

11. FIND THE GOLD UNDER THE SHELL

Known as the "House of the Shells", it was first an urban palace built from 1493 to 1517, in a Gothic style with Plateresque elements. It was declared a National Monument in 1929. It's now a public library. It's very close to the Plaza Mayor.

The building was built under the orders of Rodrigo Maldonado of Talavera, who was a professor and dean of the University. His son, Rodrigo Arias Maldonado, continued the construction. Arias Maldonado married a young aristocrat, named Juana Pimentel. The Pimentel's shield was a shell, so in a demonstration of love, the husband added the shells on the outside walls to honor his wife.

One legend has it that under one of the shells is hidden an ounce of gold. It was a common practice back then, to bring good luck upon the building. Another legend says that the family hid their jewelry under one of the shells, documenting the value but not the shell. Whoever wants to accept the challenge of finding that treasure, must contribute with the amount as a deposit. If you find the treasure, you take it and recuperate the deposit, if not, you lose it. Do you dare to try?

Michelle Torres

12. LIS' HOUSE-MUSEUM

This is an urban palace built between the end of the XIX and the beginning of the XX centuries. First conceived as the home of the businessman Miguel de Lis, the building is one of the few examples of Modernism in Salamanca.

After many owners, it finally ended in the city town hall's hands, who restored it and made a museum out of it, about Art Nouveau and Deco.

The Lis' House Museum of Art Nouveau and Deco shows samples of decorative objects between the last decades of the XIX and the World War II. Its windows are decorated with colorful designs.

There are rooms with art collections, and a coffee shop where you can sit and enjoy comfortably the place after touring the museum.

13. THE GARDEN OF CALISTO AND MELIBEA

This garden, inaugurated in 1981, is located in the Old Town of Salamanca, near the Tormes river. The name is due to the main characters of a novel written by Fernando de Rojas, "The Celestine", in 1502.

It's believed that there was the place were Calisto and Melibea used to meet to share their love and at the end of the novel (spoiler alert) end their lives. It's common for couples to walk through this garden, sit, chat and enjoy the view of the city.

There's an usual practice where the lovers lock a padlock in the well, as a proof of their love. I strongly recommend you not to, because it damages the structure. The idea is to enjoy the place and leave it in the best conditions possible, for upcoming tourists!

14. SCALA COELI'S TOUR

Also known as "La Clerecía", this building was constructed between the XVII and XVIII centuries to be the "Royal School of the Holy Spirit", after the expulsion of Jesuits from Spain. In 1940 the Pope Pio XII decided to use the building as another University, the "Universidad Pontificia".

The tour includes access to terraces, where you'll have an amazing perspective of the structure of the building, with audio guides, exposition of paintings and real documents.

The tour begins through three halls, with different stories within them. It ends with the main thing; the towers and the bell tower. You'll have a spectacular view of the city's Old Town.

15. Beware Of The Devil In The Cave

The Salamanca's Cave is a crypt left of what was Saint Cebrian's Church, demolished in the XVI century. The legend says that Hercules founded an academy to teach magic, but apparently one of the professors was the devil, who taught necromancy every night for seven years to seven disciples. When they finished the career, one of them had to stay with the demon, but one of the students fooled him and could escape.

The city of Salamanca was considered by the obscurantism as a capital for necromantic practices. Nowadays, some Latin American countries use the word "Salamanca" to describe a cave where the demon lives or malefic forces take place.

The cave is open for tourists, with guided visits and sometimes a group of actors performs the story to amuse the visitors.

16. THE HOUSE OF THE DEATHS

This house was built in 1500. The most relevant characteristic of it is the four skulls decorating the windows of its front. It was built by Archbishop Fonseca back then and has some gore legends explaining the presence of skulls.

In the early XIX century, four people living there were brutally murdered. A few years later, a young lady who lived there fired her maids and months after, was found dead in the courtyard of the house. Also, the family of a priest was found dead in the depth of a well inside the house. A lot of souls in such a little place.

The legend has it that at night, you can hear screams of the souls there and chains dragged on the floor. Pay attention at the skulls, why are they smiling?

17. LAS DUEÑAS' CONVENT

This building is one of the biggest jewels of Spanish Renaissance. Built in 1553, the "Santa Maria de la Consolacion" (Holy Mary of Consolation) convent was exclusively inhabited by Dominica's nuns until 1962, when the building is first opened for tourists.

It's a Grotesque-style construction, with different and very detailed carvings in each column, that sums up the beliefs and myths of that epoch. There's a carving of Dante Alighieri's face, can you find him?

Back then, the cloister was meant for nobility women, aristocrat widows and wives of knights (while their husbands were at war). They came here to devote their lives to God but keeping contact with the world, making vows of obedience and celibacy, but not of poverty. Even the richest brought their maids. Because of the high social hierarchy of these women, people in town started to call this building "Las Dueñas' Convent" ("Las Dueñas'" means "The Owners").

18. San Esteban's Convent

The Convent of San Esteban was a center for studying and teaching Theology. Here, in 1299, was established the General Centre of Studies for the Dominicans in Spain. In 1509, the friars of this Convent decided to commit themselves to the missionary task in the new lands recently discovered in America. To this convent belongs the first Dominicans that arrived at the Island of La Española (or Hispaniola, also called the Island of St. Dominic – what is today Haiti and the Dominican Republic) in mid-September of 1510. The building itself begins its construction in 1524, ending in 1610.

According to tradition, Columbus stayed here before traveling to America, in his attempt to convince the geographers of the University that the journey was possible. Close to the Convent you'll find the Columbus Square, dedicated to the traveler.

Nowadays, it still works as a center of theology studies, with its own publishing house. Tourists can visit, it's open every day. The price per adult is 3€.

19. La Salina's Palace

This palace, also known as "Fonseca Palace" was built in 1538 by a nobility family, the Messia-Fonseca's. Its structure looks more like a public building than a residential one. The name "La Salina" is due to the monopoly of salt the owners had back then; that palace was the headquarter of salt-storage, until 1870.

It's built with a Plateresque style, with an inside gallery held by some tormented characters. A legend says that the Archbishop Alonso de Fonseca (the same guy that built the House of the Deaths) came to town for a few days to be in a diocesan meeting, accompanied by his lover, Juana Pimentel, also known as "La Salina". The Archbishop asked for shelter to different wealthy families of Salamanca, but they denied it because of the presence of La Salina. Apparently, Archbishop Fonseca got so angry he decided to build La Salina palace with some decoration that would represent the nobility of Salamanca in a monstrous way, carrying the walls.

20. MONTERREY'S PALACE

This palace is one of the maximum exponents of the Plateresque style in Spain. It was admired and very imitated in the XIX century. It started an artistic movement known as "Monterrey" or "Neoplateresque". It's considered the most popular Renacentist construction in Spain and Latin America. The towers and the decoration of the palace symbolizes the nobility of the Spanish Gold Era.

The building was built by the III count of Monterrey. The construction started in 1539 and stopped a few years later. The project wasn't finished. It was meant to be a (way) bigger place, and by the time they decided to build again, the area they planned to use had other purposes.

It was declared a National Monument in 1929. Nowadays, the owners are the Alba's House (a wealthy Spanish family), and the palace is one of the places where they keep some of their collection of valuable paintings. The place is open to tourists every day of the week.

21. EL CLAVERO TOWER

This is one of the most forgotten and emblematic things to see in Salamanca. Drowning in the streets and modern buildings, El Clavero Tower stands out with its 20 meters of height and its fortress-like construction, with an octagonal shape.

It was built in the second half of the XV century, by "El Clavero" Don Francisco of Sotomayor. "El Clavero" was the man responsible for the custody of the Christ's nails in the processions, the offerings and religious acts. He was also responsible for the keys of the archive and the belongings of the Order of Alcántara back then. The tower's name is due to the responsibilities of Sotomayor as "El Clavero". The Order is a military and religious order created in 1154, which still endures nowadays.

The Tower was declared a National Monument in 1931.
□□

Don't forget to take a good picture of this remaining piece of history, forgotten within the streets of Salamanca.

22. TENTENECIO STREET

This is a beautiful street that used to connect the Roman bridge with the Old Cathedral in older times. It's in the historic center of the city. It once was the main road to enter Salamanca from the South. Nowadays it's a pedestrian street but has some restricted traffic.

The street is named due to a miracle did there from Saint Juan de Sahagun, the Saint patron of the city. He was an Augustin fray, famous for his miracles.

Before its current name, the street was called "Saint Catalina". The legend has it that a bull escaped, panicking the city. Sahagun was taking a walk, or maybe spending time with his congregation, in this street when he saw the animal running. To save the people there, he screamed: "Stop, fool!" (the traduction of " 'tente (detente), necio!"), and the 500 kg-beast instantly stopped.

This street is a must when you come visit if you want to feel the Salamantine vibe in all its way.

23. THE MARIQUELO

If you visit in October, you can't miss this. The Mariquelos were a family that lived in the Cathedral, in charge of ringing the bell when needed. The 31st of October, in the year 1755, happened a very strong earthquake, known as the "Lisbon Earthquake". It had a magnitude of 9 (Richter scale) and provoked a tsunami that affected a good part of Western Europe and Northern Africa. It destroyed the Portuguese capital, Lisbon. Because of its proximity to the devastated city, Salamanca also felt the earthquake effects, and the population sheltered in the New Cathedral. The construction was almost intact after the event. The most damaged structure was the tower, that was slightly inclined. One of the Mariquelos climbed up to the tower to check the inclination and plan further repairs.

As a commemoration of that day, every 31st of October someone would climb the tower to ring the bell, thank God and ask him to prevent the event from happening again. Besides, someone had to climb to check if the tower was in its position. The people in charge of starting this tradition were the Mariquelo family. The last authentic Mariquelo climbed the tower until 1977. In 1985 the tradition was rescued again and is still practiced nowadays. Every 31st of October the Mariquelo climbs the tower of the Cathedral dressed as a Charro, and plays music with typical Salamantine's instruments.

24. BUY YOUR GOODS AT THE CENTRAL MARKET

This market is the place you have to go if you want to buy typical ingredients of Salamanca's gastronomy. It's right next to the Plaza Mayor. It's origins go back to the XII and XIII centuries.

Originally placed next to the Old Cathedral, after a while the market is moved to the location it has nowadays. The Town Hall was responsible for the food distribution in the city during the XVIII century. At the end of the XIX century, the idea was born to give the Salamantines a roofed market, so the Town Hall had a contest for architects, where the winning prize was building that structure. The contest was won by the same architect who designed the Lis' House, Joaquin Vargas y Aguirre. The building was built between 1899 and 1909; economic problems delayed the construction for eleven years. It was finally inaugurated in April 1909.

If you want to eat the autochthonous Salamanca's food, when you arrive at the market ask for: "Morucha" meat; "Charra" veal; "Guijuelo" ham; "Arribes" cheese and "Fuentesauco" chickpeas.

You'll have a feast at the "charro" way!

25. Buy An Ice-Cream In "La Novelty"

"La Novelty" is a cafe in located in the Plaza Mayor. It has more than a hundred years (it was inaugurated in 1905). If you want a taste of Salamanca's history, this place is a must.

Miguel de Unamuno (philosopher and writer) came every day to have bull sessions. Ortega y Gasset, Antonio Tovar, Vargas Llosa... Even the king Alfonso XIII and dictator Franco came to this place. Here, famous writers, artists, politicians, and scientifics had seat to chat and share ideas. There's a statue in Torrente Ballester's honor (another famous writer and professor) sitting in one of the tables, so you can sit with him as well.

This place is famous for its coffee (I recommend you their Irish Coffee) and its wine, but mostly for the ice cream. They craft their own ice creams since its inauguration, and every year they create a new flavor, such as chocolate with bitter orange or cheese with cranberries. They make special ice creams for Christmas as well.

Michelle Torres

26. LEAVE A POST-IT AT PANCAKE CAFE & TE

This place brags that "Unamuno never had a coffee here". The Pancake cafe & te is one little coffee shop near the House of the Shells.

It has amazing coffee and pastry, with vegan options. You have to pay in cash and it's so tiny you will probably like to have it to go. But while you're waiting, you can check the wall. It's filled with post-its of the clients.

Their pizza is amazing and their "pancake iced coffee" too. This place is considered the best "take away" of Salamanca, compared to the Starbucks franchise.

Make sure to buy a good coffee or tea to go, leave a post-it and keep touring the city!

27. RESTAURANTS, PART I

If you're a sybarite, here's a list of some good and elegant restaurants in Salamanca:

Casa Paca: This is a Salamanca's classic. They have many options on their menu (including vegetarian meals) but their strength relies on the meat preparations.

Vinodiario: Another classic in town. This place is famous for their tapas and wine-tasting. They have vegetarian and vegan options as well.

La Hoja 21: This place offers traditional food with an 'avant-garde" touch. They have vegetarian and vegan options.

Victor Gutierrez' Restaurant: Victor Gutierrez is a Peruvian chef with a Michelin star. He presents a fusion cuisine with Spanish and Peruvian that will give you a memorable experience.

En La Parra: Here they offer European and Spanish cuisine. They have gluten-free options. It's a cozy and small place to eat comfortably.

El Mesón de Gonzalo: They offer Mediterranean and Spanish dishes. Don't forget to have the roasted artichokes for entry and torrijas for dessert.

28. Restaurants, Part II + Vegan Options

If you want to have an amazing meal but don't care about Michelin stars or fancy places, here's another list:

Viandas de Salamanca: They have many (MANY) iberic snacks to offer, mostly with different kinds of ham.

Mesón Los Faroles: This place in Van Dyck's street uses to be very crowded. The tapas and drinks are excellent.

La Viga: They're famous for their "jeta", a piece from the pork's snout.

Gran Tasca Bar Manzano: They offer a wide menu of tapas, and even though it might be crowded, the attention from the waiters won't let you down.

Café de Chinitas: This is in Van Dyck's too. Their meals are delicious but don't forget to ask for the mushrooms' brochette.

For vegans:

Cafe Atelier: They offer meals during the day and tapas at night. Their home-made dishes are delicious.

269 Gastro Vegan: This is a very cozy place with original decoration (forms of livestock animals on the walls made with fake grass). The food is amazing and the attention is 10/10.

29. HAVE A MEAL AT "LA CABALLERIZA"

This is, nowadays, the cafeteria of the Filology Faculty. You enter at "Las Caballerizas" through a little door, kind of hidden, in Tostado street. If you get lost, don't be shy and ask; every Salamantino knows where this place is.

It was built in the XVII century as a stable (Stable in Spanish is "caballeriza"). Afterwards, it was the storage room of the Teacher's School and in the Spanish Civil War, it was an anti-bomb shelter. The place was forgotten until 1970 when the building was restored and Las Caballerizas opened as a cafeteria. The place is preserved as it was originally, with its bricks and characteristic vaults. Joaquín Sabina, Jesús Hermida, Juan Echanove, the Hurtado Sisters and even Princess Leticia have been here. The proof is in the pictures the owners keep on the walls, as a mural.

Please don't forget to ask for the "embutido ibérico". You can ask for tapas, like "hormigón universitario" (university's concrete), which is a delicious tortilla they make. All the food is homemade, as it was 30 years ago when they started.

Michelle Torres

30. TASTE THE "HORNAZO" IN THE LUNES DE AGUA

The "Lunes de Aguas" is a traditional local festivity, where the Salamantinos gather with friends and family to have an "hornazo" outdoors. This tradition is almost exclusive of Salamanca and takes place the Monday after the Lent. This tradition goes back to the XVI century. The king Felipe II was famous for his rectitude and obedience to religion, so when he arrived in Salamanca, he was perplexed by the number of students committed to lust and alcohol. He decided to enact an edict wherein the Lent days the prohibition of meat was meant for every sense, including sexual intercourse. The prostitutes were expelled from the town within that period of time. When the Lent ended, that Monday the students went to the river to receive the prostitutes again with a big party. Because of the wildness of this "celebration", the church forbid it, but the tradition remained. Nowadays, the Lunes de Aguas is celebrated mostly with the Hornazo, a representative food of Salamanca (it has quality standard and certain regulations to be made). The Hornazo has different kinds of meat, like sausage, ham, and loin. Sometimes, boiled eggs. Whether you are in town for the Lunes de Aguas or not, don't forget to have a taste of a Salamantine's Hornazo!

31. VIRGEN DE LA VEGA'S FESTIVAL

Every 8th of September, Salamanca celebrates the Festival of the Virgin de la Vega. This tradition began long ago as a livestock fair, but nowadays is a big festival to celebrate the Virgin, taking place every year.

The legend says that the Virgin helped Salamanca in the attempted assault of the invader troops in 1706 during the War of Spanish Succession. A statue representing the Virgin was recovered from the Monastery of Vega and was placed in the Cathedral of Salamanca. The Virgin has been the Saint of the city since 1618 and shares this patronage with San Juan de Sahagun. There have been several miracles and favors attributed to her intervention.

The festival usually lasts a week, with shows in the streets, concerts, food stands in many streets, cultural activities and parties for citizens, students, and tourists. A schedule of events is published in the news and on the streets. The town gets crowded with visitors coming from all over the country to enjoy this festival, which also takes place close to the end of school vacations.

32. Brunch At Mandala

Here you can eat at any time of the day, but I love to have a nice brunch in this place. They offer tasty vegetarian options, but they're famous for their tortillas, fruit smoothies, and home-made cakes. They have a lot of teas to choose from as well.

If you want to have an afternoon snack, I recommend you the "Muerte de chocolate" (Chocolate Death) cake with a good smoothie.

The waiters are amazing, always smiling. The decoration is based on India, with elephants and a Buddha statue. It's colorful but peaceful at the same time.

This place is very close to Plaza Mayor, right in front of the Universidad Pontificia. It gets very crowded sometimes, so make sure to make a reservation before.

They offer combo-meals of: 1st and 2nd dish + bread + water, or beer, or wine + dessert or coffee for a few € (10 to 12 €). They offer these combos on weekends but +2 or 3€ than the normal prize.

33. GO TAPA'S

One of the most popular things to do in Spain is "going to tapas" or "tapear". This is visiting as many restaurants as you can, having appetizers and drinking wine with friends.

If you want to go tapas like the best Salamantine student, you have to go to Van Dyck's Street. The street is very close to the Old Town, 10 minutes walking. The most famous places are "Café Chinitas", "El Minutejo", "Rufo's" and "El Tenderete". The fun thing about Van Dyck's is that you can eat like a king with the budget of a student. Each tapa is delicious and costs 1-2€, depending on the place and the ingredients.

34. Go Drinking

(Please, don't drink if you're underage and always stick to your group. Drink water and eat before drinking alcohol)

If you want to have a nice drink with friends or something before partying, I personally recommend you to go to:

La Chupiteria: If you like drinks in shots, this is the place. Every shot costs 1€ give or take. If you are the kind of person that really likes adrenaline, this place can offer it in two ways: The Red Devil and The Green Devil. These shots are the characteristic of this place and are a must if you're in town. The Red Devil is a mix of absinthe and ginseng. The Green is absinthe and cannabis. The absinthe itself has at least 45-75% ABV, so be careful.

Tio Vivo: This bar, very close to the Plaza Mayor, might as well be a museum. It's decorated as a carousel and has an exposition of antiques on its walls and in the place in general. You'll surely spend more time checking the original decoration than choosing what to drink. Depending on the hour, you can have tea, coffee, hot chocolate or an alcoholic drink. They have live music on Fridays, DJ presentations, and plays as well. The tables are candle-lighted, which makes it a very cozy place. The drinks are amazing and if you are a peanut lover, you can eat as much as you want for free. They have the peanuts in a big trunk, so feel free to grab as much as you like.

35. GO PARTY

As a student's city, there's no lack of places to go party. The most popular in Salamanca are:

Camelot: It opened in 1986. Has a very wide space and good music. They do concerts, different kinds of parties (for university graduates) and even a beer pong contest.

Cum Laude: This place looks like a tiny Plaza Mayor, with good music and drinks as well. It has dress code.

Posada Las Animas: There's an Animas' cafe-pub and an Animas' Disco. Both are very famous here if you want to go tapas with good music or party with your friends.

Garamond: Its pub has medieval ambiance. It's a place to eat and drink, have a nice afternoon or night with good music. The disco is open even when the others are closed. You can party there until 6 am.

Michelle Torres

36. GO SHOPPING IN TORO STREET

This is one of the pedestrian arteries of Salamanca, with famous clothing stores, markets and so on. Most of the people go shopping here. The thing is that, as everything in Salamanca, it has a history.

The Zara's building was a convent, the "Convent of Saint Anthony The Royal", of Franciscans, built in 1745.The construction wasn't completed, but the rests remained until these days. The investment in the restore of the building kept the vault of the old church. Inside, you won't be sure if you should look at the clothes or admire the walls and the roof. It's considered a Good of Cultural Interest since 1997.

37. Watch Performances At La Malhablada

If you are fond of culture and fine arts, this is the place. La Malhablada is a cultural center in the middle of Salamanca's Old Town. It's in what once was a house, built in 1908. It has a terrace with a very good view as well.

They sell artwork of different modern painters, but their strength relies on plays. There's a schedule of "microteatro" (short plays) that is changed every month. They offer a tour inside the building, talks and art expositions.

There's a coffee shop if you want to sit and enjoy the cultural environment. They open from Tuesday to Sunday.

Michelle Torres

38. Urban Gallery On The West Side

Even though Salamanca is a city known because of its history, it's looking for ways to modernize itself as well. The Urban Gallery on the West Side of the town is its best example. It is at 10 minutes walking from the Plaza Mayor.

The West Side of Salamanca doesn't have any touristic attraction, it was deteriorating and abandoned until 2013. The Neighbours Association, working together with some artists decided to start this project where paintings would be shown on the walls, garage doors, even buildings, mixing the artistic side of graffitis with tourism.

It was born as an experiment, but now over 100 paintings have been shown. Every year, mostly in June, there's a contest where young professionals, art students or amateur painters show their ideas. The winners paint their artwork on the west side on October/November. The sponsors also invite a professional artist to paint a bigger wall. It has a free mobile application and there are guided tours every Saturday at midday, 5€ per person.

39. MIGUEL DE UNAMUNO'S HOUSE-MUSEUM

The House-Museum of Miguel de Unamuno is a house located in the center of Salamanca. He was a Spanish writer and philosopher, famous for his novels, essays, plays, and poems. He wrote most of his lifework within those walls. He was dean of the University three times, from 1900 to 1936, when dictator Franco destitute him from his charge.

The house is owned by the University of Salamanca and was built in the XVIII century (between the years of 1758 to 1762), with a Baroque style. It was meant as a residence for the dean.

Since the middle of the last century, this building is dedicated to the life of Unamuno in the form of a museum. The place has objects, his personal collection of over 6,000 books, furniture and other things that belonged to him. They offer expositions of his work, as well as other patrimonial goods from Salamanca.

The museum is open from Monday to Friday, from 10 to 14.

Michelle Torres

40. LEARN ABOUT THE SPANISH CIVIL WAR AT THE ARCHIVE MUSEUM

Not visiting this museum is ignoring a very important segment of the Modern Spanish history. While Franco's dictatorship, thousands of documents were kidnapped to repress and judge the Republican enemies. Some were destroyed in the last days of the war, but some of those that remained are kept in this museum, inaugurated in 1999. The origins of this museum go back to the Spanish Civil War. Salamanca was the headquarter of Franco during the War. The Franquists needed a safe place to gather the documentation collected around the country to identify enemies and people against the ideas of the regimen. Nowadays, these documents are a valuable source for historians and even for some Republican military to request compensation for the time they spent in prison. The Archive's Museum has an area dedicated to masonry as well, with a Lodge in scale and expositions about it. Franco chased and kill Freemasons due to their beliefs and rituals, so the Archive decided to dedicate an area to learn about Masons. The entrance is free, from Tuesdays to Sundays, from 12 to 8 PM. During visiting hours, you can watch two audiovisuals; one about the history of the Archive and another about general information about masonry.

41. VISIT THE MUSEUM OF HISTORY OF AUTOMOTIVE

Located in front of Lis' House and next to the Tormes' River, the Museum of History of Automotive is the first public museum dedicated to cars in Spain. It was inaugurated in 2002 and has over 200 historic cars to show. Some of them are unique. Also, the museum has an exposition of thousands of accessories related to vehicles.

The vehicles shown are from different epochs, since before the automotive history began. You'll see inventions as well, like the first vehicle with an explosive motor of history: the tricycle of Benz. The museum presents the evolution of the vehicle production, including design tendencies and improvements in security. The exposition ends with examples of race vehicles driven by recent world champions of Formula 1.

After the visit, you can take pictures inside a vehicle and buy souvenirs.

It's opened from Tuesday to Sunday, from 10 AM to 2 PM and from 5 PM to 8 PM.

You can buy a ticket for 4 € in the Tourism Office in Plaza Mayor, that allows you to visit the Lis' House and this museum as well.

Michelle Torres

42. Bullfighting Museum

There are few things considered more traditional in Spain than bullfighting. This museum is dedicated to this world.

The museum was born to acknowledge the bullfighting itself as a tradition in Spain, as well as the bullfighters in the history of Salamanca. It was inaugurated in December of 1993 and has many rooms showing typical clothes and other assets.

Bullfighting is an activity that apparently started in the Bronze Age (about 5000 years ago), developing over the centuries as a proof of courage. It's become a tradition in Spain, with rituals and cultural background, involving the clothes of the bullfighters and the breeding of the bulls.

It's opened from Tuesday to Saturday, from 10.30 AM to 1:30 PM and from 5.30 PM to 8 PM, 3 € per person.

It's a very interesting museum to visit if you want to learn more about the history and traditions of Spain.

43. San Vicente Hill's Deposit

Here are the very roots of Salamanca. This archeological park, the "San Vicente Hill" park, has the remains of the first village in the city. The first inhabitants were here in the Iron Age.

The tour will show you where, when and why the city was born. You'll see actual remains of the village and the visit will be guided by archeologists who participated in the restore of the remains. You'll walk the hill, where you'll have one of the most amazing views of Salamanca. There's a wide space showing the exhumed remains of the archeological excavations, which correspond to a part of the village that lived at San Vicente Hill between the VII and IV centuries before Christ.

The visit lasts 2 hours. If you're interested, go to the Office of Touristic Information in the Plaza Mayor to know the visiting hours.

It's crazy how this city has been here for more than two millennia. This is a very interesting tour. Don't miss the chance to check this place out!

44. Jesuita's Park

This park, in the middle of the city, has almost 100 000 square meters. It is the lung of Salamanca.

It once was a garden owned by the Jesuits. They used to grow food and have livestock there. The land was given to the Town Hall in the early 80's under the condition that a common area was made there.

The park has been restored a few times since then. Now, it has three playgrounds for kids, one for dogs, a lake with ducks, exercise areas, a walking and biking route inside, as well as a coffee shop and plenty of places to sit. If you like to keep contact with the mother nature without leaving town, this is an amazing option for you.

45. La Almedilla Park

This is a park near the center of Salamanca, built by the Town Hall in the late 1800's. It was originally meant to be a livestock area, but the governors back then decided to build another place for the Salamantinos to meet instead of the Plaza Mayor.

They built this park, trying to make it as beautiful and green as possible, including a lake and a mini-zoo, but people didn't get used to it and decided to remain in the Plaza Mayor. In the mid-1900's the park got famous again, and nowadays it's a very popular place.

You can have a picnic near the lake while watching the swans, ducks, and gooses, with your lover or with your children. There's also an exercise area and water springs.

46. La Aldehuela And El Baldío Park

If you're worried about keeping your training schedule, there's La Aldehuela. It is a "sports city", with over 200 km2 dedicated exclusively for training. It has a gym, numerous courts for soccer, tennis, volleyball and even one for rugby. It has running racks and a skate park, so whichever sport you're into, you won't have the problem to keep accomplishing your fitness goals. It's opened from 8 AM to 11 PM on weekdays and from 9 AM to 9 PM on weekends.

If you're traveling with your dog, there's El Baldio park. It's a park dedicated exclusively to this beautiful pets. It has over 150 km2 for your dog to run safely without its leash. It has a fountain so you don't have to worry about bringing bottles to keep you and your pet hydrated.

47. RECEIVE THE NEW YEAR WITH THE UNIVERSITY GRADS

Every last Thursday of the academic year, the students gather in Plaza Mayor to celebrate the New Year in advance. This started in 1999 when a group of university students met to simulate the 12 bell tolls that receive the upcoming year because in the real day they would be with their families, and wouldn't be able to share that moment with their classmates or roommates. They "received" the New Year together with jelly beans instead of grapes.

They repeated it year after year, inviting friends and more classmates until it became what it is nowadays: an event of over 40,000 students receiving the upcoming year, together, two weeks in advance. The event organizers also set up a route to the discos to end the night partying.

If you plan to receive the New Year here, this is a must!

Michelle Torres

48. San Silvestre Salamantina

The "San Silvestre" is a famous worldwide race done the last Sunday of the year, in the Saint's honor (even though he wasn't a runner or athlete himself).

The first San Silvestre in Salamanca was in 1984, with 389 contestants. By 2017, the number of runners expected is over 7,000. There are four different routes, the longest is almost 3km long. Adults, kids, and athletes run this every year, it's a very "healthy" way to end the year and tour the city.

The race has prices for the winners in its different categories. Also, contests of best costumes, posters and even short stories with prices for the winners as well.

49. GO WALKING EVERYWHERE

One of the best things about Salamanca is that you can go almost everywhere walking. The city feels like it was made for that. The sidewalks are wide, there are many trees and parks, as well as a coffee shop almost in every corner to rest from touring. Also, all the buildings you'll visit are very close to each other. Most of them are in the surroundings of the Plaza Mayor, so it's worth walking. Maybe in one of those walks around the House of The Shells or Toro Street, you'll listen to Michael. He's a violinist that has been living in the city for over ten years and plays beautifully. There's an accordionist who plays songs of Carlos Gardel (the Argentinian tango singer) and two brothers that perform with puppets playing instruments near the Plaza Mayor. No matter if you're inside a building touring the history of Salamanca or taking pictures of the Cathedrals, you can always meet with one of these musicians on the street and enjoy the walk with the perfect background music. If you are more the bicycle-kind of person, there are several points in the city where you can rent a bicycle, tour and return it to another rent point. There are plenty of routes for cyclists as well. If you're feeling lazy you can always take the bus. It covers plenty of routes so it will take you everywhere. Also, if you're planning to have a meeting with someone, do it the Salamantine way: meet under the clock of the Plaza Mayor.

50. LOOKING FOR SOUVENIRS?

Besides the classic **frog-key chain** or the **University hoodie or shirt,** there are other things you could take with you as amazing souvenirs:

- **Filigree Charra**. This is a metalwork technique where fine threads of metal (usually gold or silver) are intertwined to create jewelry. The "charro button" is an ornament of the classic suit of charros. If you want to take something truly Salamantine, take one of these with you. There are some good jewelry shops in the Plaza Mayor.

- **Food.** Don't forget to take a Guijuelo ham and or a hornazo back home. You'll miss them. Also, you can do the last visit to the Central Market to buy your favorite goods.

- **A Su Gusto Jabones**. This little shop is famous locally because it has a collection of colorful edible-looking handmade soaps. This could be a good gift for a loved one!

- **El Rastro.** If you want to have options because you have no idea what to bring home, go to El Rastro. It's a flea market done every Sunday in front of La Aldehuela park. I'm sure you'll find what you're looking for there.

- There are shops where you can buy beautiful fans, magnets, shirts or handmade cups decorated with the amazing views of the city. Also, you can buy something more Salamantine, like a charro suit.

>TOURIST

Michelle Torres

TOP REASONS TO BOOK THIS TRIP

1) It's a World Heritage Site, declared by the UNESCO. Does that need further explanation?

2) It's a place filled with history and traditions. Every corner has a story to tell.

3) Charros are one of the most gentle and nice people you'll ever meet. If you meet one (I'm sure you will) you'll have the best tourist guide ever.

4) The food is delicious. Really. It doesn't matter if you go to a fancy restaurant or to Van Dyck's, the food will always be amazing.

5) Everything is close, at walking distance. Also, you can rent a bike or if you're feeling lazy, the bus will take you anywhere.

Michelle Torres

> TOURIST
GREATER THAN A TOURIST

Visit GreaterThanATourist.com:
http://GreaterThanATourist.com

Sign up for the Greater Than a Tourist Newsletter:
http://eepurl.com/cxspyf

Follow us on Facebook:
https://www.facebook.com/GreaterThanATourist

Follow us on Pinterest:
http://pinterest.com/GreaterThanATourist

Follow us on Instagram:
http://Instagram.com/GreaterThanATourist

Michelle Torres

> TOURIST
GREATER THAN A TOURIST

Please leave your honest review of this book on Amazon and Goodreads. Thank you.

We appreciate your positive and negative feedback as we try to provide tourist guidance in their next trip from a local.

Michelle Torres

NOTES

Printed in Great Britain
by Amazon